I0177369

Let. Love. Speak

Book 1

Let. Love. Speak
Book 1

Maria Velazco

Copyright © 2025 by **Let.Love.Speak**

All rights reserved. No part of this publication may be reproduced in whole or in part, or stored in a retrieval system, or transmitted in any form or by any means, electronic, mechanical, photocopying, recording, or otherwise, without written permission of the publisher except for the use of brief quotations in a book review or scholarly journal.

First Printing: 2018
ISBN-13: 978-1-7324923-0-1
Let.Love.Speak
Long Beach, California

Cover Illustration by Julia O. Bianco
Back photo by Charlie Esquivias

Dedication

This book is a dream in the making, it all started with the idea of sharing the words that were stirring inside me that wanted to live on the outside. I started a blog with just that intention; I didn't conceive that it would be what you now see. I am grateful for the blessings of blind faith; taking one step at a time, not knowing what was coming. I am grateful for the prayers that brought this forth and for the time on this earth. It's time has come, it is here for you, blessings divine One.

I dedicate this book to my divine brothers and sisters, especially my siblings. Believe in yourselves, work diligently, commit, and you will achieve. I created this with the awareness that I could not ask of you that, which I myself would not do. Here it is, now go, create your dreams!

Thank you dream maker!

A note to the reader: The titles in this book are followed by the date (yr/mo/day) and time in which they were first published online.

Contents

Dream team - 2017-01-03 20:44

I'm weaving my dream
Because life's supreme
Angels in my team
In love I beam

A story - 2017-01-07 22:13

Stories of the mind
don't let them confine
Stories of the heart
those are art

Death bed - 2017-01-15 20:10

Death is a lie
before your eye
Death does not lie
where you lie

Live or die - 2017-01-17 22:03

One can die in the blink of an eye
Oh, but why do we do cry?
Is it loss? Perhaps regret?
Lots of needs never met
But let's not forget
The worst is neglect
A neglected life never lived

Courage has no armor - 2017-01-20 21:36

I have nothing to defend
need not pretend
fear is a beast
courage has no armor
love sets me free
I live in liberty

Hold love near - 2017-01-24 21:19

Fear robs you of what's here
Fear steals what is dear
Fear, I vanish you from here!
I will hold love dear
to keep fear far from here

Blessed - 2017-01-26 20:49

I am blessed to have lived, if only for a
day, in the rain.

I am blessed to have been graced, by the
embrace, of love.

I am blessed to have felt the rays, so
tenderly on my face, of the sun.

On the wings of butterflies - 2017-02-01
22:14

Prayers on the wings of butterflies
Silence in the desert air
Dreams on gleaming stars
Destiny in the child's heart

Guiding light - 2017-02-02 22:08

I praise the light within my life, my life
is that which I praise.
Dreams that I hold, never been told.
To trust my heart, that is my art.

Speak from light - 2017-02-04 21:58

Blind from what's divine are those that
seek to divide.
Unkind and in a bind are those that
speak from mind.
Awake and divine are those that unite.
Kind and free are those that speak of
light.

Part 1-I pray - 2017-02-07 20:35

To the guiding light of my day- I pray.
To the life that gives- I pray.
To the truth of all,
and to the time of all,
I pray.

Part 2-I pray - 2017-02-08 22:47

That as I run and play, don't let me
stray.
That I remain true to my heart,
that I may listen to your whispers,
as I live this life,
and as I pray, I know all will be okay.

When she falls in love - 2017-02-09
21:33

When she falls in love with the art of her
heart.
Many mountains she will part.
When she falls in love with the breath
from her lips.
The world will be at her fingertips.

Death is a word - 2017-02-10 22:29

Death is the voice that tells you you are
worthless
Death is the moment you give up on
your dreams
Death is love not shared
Death...
Death is a word not spoken

I flew - 2017-02-17 22:08

What did I do to be blue?
Oh, I thought of things that aren't true
But then I thought of you
And my heart flew!

No longer in bed - 2017-02-19 22:38

Blue is the sky before my eye.
Green, it is not greed, it is a tree.
Yellow, something mellow.
Red, no longer in bed, nothing to dread.

Thief of time - 2017-02-22 22:04

Thief of time, thief of heart.
Thief of moments I do not wish to part.
Is it smart to break a heart?
Or is it art to know how to depart?

The golden path - 2017-02-23 22:04

The path of the light warrior is to dispel
the dark in all circumstances- yet not
relinquish its gold.
To honor the power of light, by speaking
truth.
And to be aligned with the heart, while
using the power of the mind.

Around the world - 2017-03-03 21:41

My soul has been around the world
more times than I know.

Yet what my eyes behold, my heart
foretold.

Woman of bliss - 2017-03-08 22:30

Woman divine, woman sublime, you are
art.
Woman of art, woman of heart, you are
bliss.
Woman of bliss, woman of glitz, you are
free!

My refuge - 2017-03-18 22:41

My heart, my refuge.
The light, my guide.
The dark, my balance.
Life, my school.

Growing up - 2017-03-24 21:47

I was a wonder in her eye
Until I came to be
But alas she could not see
That in time I would fly

For my hands - 2017-03-26 21:43

What has come has been
What will be has been
This moment-foretold
For my hands to hold

Nothing to hide - 2017-03-28 21:25

The body does not hide-what the mind
seeks to deny.
The heart will always know-what our
actions sow.
The words we speak-tomorrow will be.

Was it mine? - 2017-03-29 22:10

No trace of thought
No trace of time
How could we think that it was 'mine'?
What pleasure we seek, is lost in rhyme

In magnificence - 2017-03-30 21:39

In silent times
You are divine
In trying times
You are divine
In turbulence
Magnificence
In diligence
Transcendence

Move to the rhythm - 2017-03-31 21:27

Walk the trail until you prevail.
Swim the shore until you're restored.
Dance to the rhythm until you've
forgiven.
Sing the song until you feel strong.

Some day in May - 2017-04-06 21:43

Some day in May
I shall pray
I'll pray for the day
I'll pray for the sun
I'll pray for the years to come
Some day in May
I shall pray
I'll pray for the joy of play
I'll pray for the morning rays
But most of all
I'll pray

A river - 2017-04-07 22:24

The turning day
the calming rain
a day of play
so much to gain
a river of thought
there is no loss

Healing truth - 2017-04-11 21:22

Truth be healed,
lies revealed.
Breaking illusion,
finding solution.

Time now - 2017-04-12 22:20

Time commenced
Time stopped
Time traveled
Time paused
Time escaped
Time won

Found truth - 2017-04-13 21:12

Truth profound
Truth be found
Truth be told
Truth behold

Trying too hard - 2017-04-14 22:44

Don't try too hard,
you won't get too far.
Just learn to let go,
then it will flow.

Space time - 2017-04-18 21:44

I thrive when I'm alive
in rhyme lays my time
to hold my place
in time and space

Evolve - 2017-04-25 20:46

Learn to humanize not demonize.
Remember to feel in order to heal.
Speak of love to evolve.

Blooming beauty - 2017-04-26 22:11

She bloomed.
She withered.
Timeless beauty never shattered.

Rekindled wisdom - 2017-04-28 15:49

Let the breath of my life speak the truth
Let the steps I take lead me home
Let the silence fill me with wisdom
Let the light guide me in the dark
Let these word rekindle my fire

Raindrops - 2017-05-02 19:22

Raindrops for rainbows
Flowers for fragrance
Sunlight for sunsets

The shadows - 2017-05-04 17:20

Prisoner of the mind,
no one's so unkind.
The shadow's the madness,
voices of sadness.

What's left? - 2017-05-19 20:27

When the left becomes the right,
we've lost the fight.
When right becomes wrong,
we've lost the fight.
When violence displaces kindness,
we've lost the fight.

The purple flower riddle - 2017-05-10-17
17:22

It is like a purple flower that doesn't
know the hour.
It is like the morning light that doesn't
know midnight.
It is like the singing bird that doesn't
know meaning.
It is like the first breath that doesn't
know death.

The tongue - 2017-5-12 22:02

There are those who speak
whose hearts are weak
release poison from their tongue.
There are those who speak
whose heart is strong
their words are like a song.

Truth is strong - 2017-05-17 16:43

What sorrow comes that lasts until
morrow?
What madness speaks that love is bleak?
What chains take hold that no one's
bold?
'The truth is strong,' goes our song.
Love's not frail-it will prevail.
The day will come when all will hail-'We
are One!'

The clock's time - 2017-05-23 21:59

The time on the clock is not the time
The end of the day is not the end
The clock's time is not the clock's
The end of the day is not the day's

Travel light - 2017-06-02 21:46

Live light
Be bold
Time nothing
Love greatly

Flying soon Part 1 - 2017-06-07 17:16

On survival mode,
don't know how to let go mode.
Trapped for so long,
forgotten where I belong.
Said I was strong,
don't know where I went wrong.
Want to let go,
but how? I don't know.
Freedom's forgotten,
chains begotten.
Learning to be free,
and how to be me.
Crying but not dying,
soon I'll be flying!

Flying soon Part 2 - 2017-06-08 21:57

I'm flying,
done crying.
Love's a token,
truth be spoken,
heart's not broken.

The witches cackle - 2017-06-13 21:22

Laughter fills the air,
for we -the great heirs
of wisdom, wonder
and all yonder.

It is not what our eyes believe,
but rather -what our hearts perceive.

Truth profound,
loves the sound,
of all that is, and all that was,
the witches cackle homeward bound.

To my brothers - 2017-06-14 22:31

My darling brothers,
Cherish your tears,
release your fears.
Your heart is gold,
remove your blindfold.
Lift your light,
no need to fight.
Truth's a ladder,
nothing else matters.

Arriving - 2017-06-15 22:37

Still on earth
everyday a birth
Living a dream
on a light stream
Finally arriving
no longer surviving
Challenging comfort
enjoying discomfort
Peace is a journey
of that you are worthy

The river - 2017-06-17 22:40

To the river I shall go,
and release all I know.
Ever flowing, trust bestowing,
sunlit river, growing, flowing.

Flowing energy - 2017-06-23 21:00

A life that flows is a life that grows.
Love that's shared shows you cared.
Words that are honored shows what you
valued.

Dear sister - 2017-06-27 21:55

I am sorry that there weren't people to help you see your divine nature.

I am sorry for those who turned a blind eye when you were in pain.

I am sorry for the times you may have fallen and forgotten who you are.

I am sorry for all the pain that you are going through-I see you, I see who you are, and I love you.

May you have the courage to stand up to your demons, may you find the light within your life.

May you soar with the wind and roar with the fire, may the water cleanse your soul and the earth cradle you more.

May life be a venture into the depths of your soul, and may our friendship be fuel for your light, I will love you ever more.

Rain - 2016-01-29 15:22

If you see me outside, I have a smile on
my face so that I look like I belong.
But if you look inside my heart, you will
find I'm falling apart.
There's a pain inside that is tearing me
apart.
Inside this space, there is also a yearning
to belong.
I long to see the rainbow on the other
side.
Cause I'm hoping for peace on the
inside.

Light - 2016-03-04 15:07

Light of love, light of will
Light of glory, light of bliss
Love of all, love of one
Love for all, love for one
Freedom of truth, freedom of desire
Freedom to dream, freedom to live
Peace is true, peace is free
Peace is light, peace is love
I AM ONE

Dance - 2016-03-14 23:24

Moving swiftly, moving quickly
Moving gently, moving softly
I dance with grace, I dance with faith
I dance with love as your divine embrace
Through the darkest days and through
the darkest nights
You are the light for all that's right

Honest - 2016-03-16 21:30

Tell the truth from the heart,
never wonder what it was,
let it go,
let it flow,
life's a wonder,
now you know.

The circle - 2016-03-17 22:50

What do you see?
Is it truly me?
Don't try to flee,
it is I you see.
I fill your days and fill your nights,
your restless search 'tis a plight.
What do you see?
It's a reflection of thee,
it is you, you see
A cycle of life
You, me, and I are One.

See me - 2016-03-29 21:06

See me walk, see me strut,
see my beauty, see my grace.
Is it me? Is it you?
Beauty lies in all our eyes.
Breathe it in, breathe it now.
Love graces all.
Am I his? Or am I hers?
I belong to all that is.

To a tree - 2016-03-31 21:20

Beloved tree, may I be as strong as thy
trunk, flexible as thy branches, and free
as thy leaves.

May I learn thy tolerance with the birds
that nest in thine branches and play
among thy leaves.

Beloved tree, let us remember to be
strong in our roots so our fruit may be
free.

Love poem - 2016-04-14 20:29

Love is an energy I use to create
Love is an energy I use to evolve
Love is what I see
Love is what I am
Love triumphs
Love heals
Love is
Love

The cycle - 2016-05-05 19:54

A joyous day, a joyous life
The darkest day, the darkest life
The spark of the moment, the spark of
life
The dimming moment, the dimming of
life
The prosperous journey, the prosperous
life
The scarcity of the journey, the scarcity
of life
The beginning of discovery, the
beginning of life
The end of discovery, the end of life

Countless - 2016-05-28 11:11

Countless ways
Countless thoughts
Countless journeys
Countless prayers
Countless tears
Countless smiles
Countless miles
The journey is not fear, nor is it the
mind
The journey is Now
Now is the journey of a thousand miles
Now is the moment of that smile
I am the life
I am the love
I am the second
I am that moment
That moment is...
Now

Love is... - 2016-05-31 19:50

Love is a gift I give myself
Love is a gift that gives me life
Love is a gift that I re-gift
Love is a gift that fills me more
Love is a gift.....there's nothing more

Angry - 2016-06-01 10:48

Angry is the heart that cannot express
Angry is the heart that is silenced
Angry is the word of those in violence
Angry is the mother of the dead
Angry is the thorn of envy
Angry is the sound of hate
Angry is and anger does
Angry is the beasts thunder

Full - 2016-06-03 16:56

Full of life, in light I live
Full of love, the treasure's within
Full of bliss, I have nothing to miss
Full of joy, I have no desire
Full of freedom, I am no slave
Full of courage, I faced my monster
Full of all that I am, I am what I am

The light in me - 2016-06-11 17:58

The happiness in me sees the happiness in you.
The love in me smiles at the love in you.
My unconditional love for you is my unconditional love for me.
My excitement for life is my excitement for your life.
The joy in me shares the joy in you.
The playfulness in me rejoices in the playfulness in you.
I have no judgment, you are my best friend.
I have no fear, I hold you dear.

Within me - 2016-06-28 10:19

Within me, there is a fire that burns, the greater the fire, the more it burns.

It burns bridges that no longer serve, habits that need be released, and karma that is no more.

The greater this fire grows the gentler I grow, for this fire knows, I flow when I let go.

Still walking - 2016-07-16 11:21

At what time does this journey stop?
Where does it end?
But most of all, when did it begin?
Is it like a river that runs through the
forest?
Or is it like a movie with a fabulous end?
Am I the director?
Or am I just a character?
Am I the beginning or am I the end?
Could I be the dog chasing its tail?
Or the apple that has fallen from the
tree?
Where does it end?

Madness is... - 2016-07-21 21:56

Madness is what you do when you don't tell the people you love that you love them.
Madness is what you do when you don't embrace the people that you love.
Madness is what you do when you keep yourself in that comfortable spot because you think it is safe, only to realize that it's what has been keeping you prisoner all along.
Madness is what occurs when you don't smile after you have fallen, because the only thing that can happen after you fall is that you can get back up.
Madness is what occurs when you don't face your biggest fear.
Madness is what happens when you keep making the same mistake over and over again because you are afraid of what other people will think... only to see that it is you who is paying the price.
This madness is sacred because it is what eventually breaks you free.

Strong enough - 2016-07-24 20:15

I am strong enough to breathe through
the madness of my thoughts.
Strong enough to see through my
challenging thoughts.
Strong enough to talk, when I'd rather
fall silent.
Strong enough to stand, when I have
fallen.
Strong as the tree.
Strong as the wind.
Strong as the river that runs through my
veins.
They are in me and I am in them.

She is beautiful - 2016-08-04 21:13

She is beautiful, she walks with her feet
bare.
She is beautiful, I try not to stare.
She is beautiful, lives life without a care.
She is beautiful, loves a good dare.
She is beautiful, spreads beauty
everywhere.
She is beautiful, her spirit rather rare.

Of all the things - 2016-08-16 13:48

Of all the things you sacrifice, don't let it
be your heart. Your heart is where I
speak to you; your heart is where I play.

Of all the things you throw away, don't
let it be your time. Your time is all I give
to you, don't throw it all away.

Of all the things you seek from me, don't
let it be more land. The land is of your
essence, experience all its presence.

My chains - 2016-08-17 22:45

I recognize the chains, they hold me
tight in their grip, suffocating the life in
me. I panic and breathe, I remember
what it was to be free. I know I have a
choice, make no change and I'll never be
free, take a breath and break the link to
set me free-I breathe- I breathe sweet
liberty, liberty to be free, liberty to be
me.

I'm ready - 2016-08-25 12:43

Ready to transcend, life doesn't end.
Ready to move on, not holding on.
Ready to fly, no need to cry.
Ready to surrender, no need to
remember.
Ready for the silence, it is my guidance.
Ready for my life, no need for strife.

Blessings - 2016-08-26 20:28

Blessing to the shelter-less man on the
street, he reminds me to be grateful.
Blessings to the darkness, it reminds me
of the light.
Blessing to the elderly, they remind me
that time is borrowed.
Blessings to illness, it reminds me of my
power to heal.
Blessing to kisses, they remind me of
sweetness.
Blessings to the child, she reminds me to
play.

Autumn Leaves - 2016-09-02 21:57

Autumn leaves find my eyes, color my
dreams, uplift my life.
Autumn leaves destined to fall, destined
to breathe.
Autumn leaves you color my heart, you
are divine art.
Autumn leaves you paint the hills and
fill the air.
Autumn leaves and winter comes.

Be - 2016-10-11 19:48

The harmony, the rhythm, it's all inside.
The truth, the wisdom, it's all divine.
The breaths that I take, the mistakes I
make, it's all in line.
The days, the years, the minutes are too.
Our heart is so simple, yet thoughts
bemuse.
Why do we seek when we just need to
be?

Silence - 2016-10-14 20:34

In this madness, in this sadness, I'm
feeling blue.
In this holy mess, during these holidays,
I still have no clue.
Thirsty, hungry, I do not feel angry.
Wandering, pondering, still have no
energy.
In everything and in nothing, just
standing here still.
Listening, dreaming, believing, it's the
silence that fills.
Yet the same silence that fills, is not the
same silence that kills.

Flipped - 2016-10-18 22:13

The hungry aren't poor
The rich not satisfied
The dark not sad
The intelligent not wise
The handicap not disabled
The capable not enabled

Food - 2016-10-20 16:50

Feed your soul, not your ego.
Feed your life, not your death.
Feed your wisdom, not your ignorance.
Feed the angels, not the demons.
Feed the truth, not the lies.
Feed the light, not the dark.

Sparkle - 2016-10-21 11:59

I am the wonderful of my life.
I am the sunshine, the sun rise.
I am the vibrant colors of the sky.
I am the sparkles and the shine.
I am the beauty of my eye.
I am divine.

Lost thought - 2016-10-26 22:23

I'm holding a thought
Keeping the pattern
Thriving a lot
Nothing to ponder
Living a lot
Wonders that matter
Stories got caught
No, I'm not lost
Wait where's that thought?

Flames - 2016-10-27 21:44

Flame of heart
Art thou art?
Flame of life
Art thou mine?
Flame of passion
Art thou action?
Flame of the night
Art thou bright?

The Present - 2016-11-01 15:47

Presence the present
The present is presence
The present is pre-sent
Presence the present

It's with my heart - 2016-11-08 21:54

It's not with my ears, you hear.
It's not with my eyes, you see.
It's not with my hands, you feel.
No, it's not with my tongue or my nose.
It's with my heart.

Focus - 2016-11-10 21:02

Focus on the light, you will be alright.
Focus on your breath, it's far from
death.
Focus on what's right, you'll have a good
night.
Focus on your dreams, they are light
beams.
Focus on the flower, it's only been an
hour.

Together - 2016-11-12 20:05

Tired of discrimination-that thing called
separation.
It's time for unity-purity of the heart.
No more segregation-let's stick together
for the nation.
No more colors-only lovers.
Let's elevate each other-no need to hate
each other.
Change is an ugly name-let's call it
progress.

Old fashioned - 2016-11-13 19:32

I'm an old fashioned gal
I prefer walks in the park
The cold hard truth over a comforting lie
A hard covered book
A man of his word, over an empty IOU
The star covered sky
Hearty home cooked meals, over frozen
dinners
I'm just an old fashioned gal

Your magic key - 2016-11-15 21:06

Don't sell yourself short, honor your
heart-set the bar-and watch the magic
unravel.
Be gentle as the painter's brush- you too
are art.
Speak your truth- no one else can do it
for you.
Don't forget who you are, the battles
you've overcome, how far you've walked.
And of course remember, you hold the
key-to set yourself free.

Still - 2016-11-25 20:28

Still your rivers
never cease
always flowing
ever growing.
Silence stills
never amiss.
Treasure trolls
all rainbows.
Ever grow
never know.

The dark side - 2016-12-01 20:33

It is best,
to be on a quest,
of self love and care.
Let us dare,
just to be fair,
to know our dark side too.
For what I see in you,
is what I carry too.

The season - 2016-12-06 20:56

The thing about the season is not the
season,
it is the feeling in the air.
A calendar date in the year,
a linear timeline for some,
an eternal moment for others.
The thing about the season is not the
season,
it is a choice of joy,
a cherished memory,
a pattern of thoughts.
The thing about the season, is that it's
not the season at all.

The temple - 2016-12-07 22:02

The temple of my heart is where I
belong.
The days are long yet my heart never
wrong.
The temple of my heart is where I
belong,
I listen to the whispers of its song.
The temple of my heart is where I
belong,
its silence invites me to play along.
The temple of my heart is where I
belong.

Tree of glee - 2016-12-08 21:12

In her thoughts are patterns of prose no
one knows,
and through the groves of trees she feels
free,
her laughter a glee,
she knows there is nothing to see,
all you have to do is be,
just like the tree, you see!

Living or fearing - 2016-12-15 21:53

Fear of feeling is fear of living
Fear of grieving is fear of living
Fear of believing is fear of living
Fear is not living
Love is living

Alive - 2016-12-25 22:43

Focus on what's alive,
from there you will thrive.
If you look at what has left,
that will be theft,
theft of the present is to focus on what's
past.
Want to grow? Learn to let go.

I am here - 2016-12-27 21:43

You see me in a leaf
You breathe me in the air
You savor me in chocolate
You harbor me in your heart
You find me in art
Yet you ask, where art thou?
Listen now, I am where thou art.

Fluttering through - 2016-12-29 21:51

Like a thought you flutter through
And in my eyes I only see you
Trust in truth
It's all in you

Blooming - 2015-07-28 19:35

I admire her beauty, her life, the joy that she brings into my life. Then I wonder what the world would look like if all the flowers decided that they didn't want to grow, that they didn't like change, and that the world was too corrupt for them to show up. We would be left without knowing the extension of God's beauty through a flower; we would never know her sweet fragrance or her vibrant colors, all because she decided that she didn't want to change because it was too scary.

I see humans like flowers, full of unlimited potential if only they would allow change to transform them, if only they would follow the light and let go of what was. Detached from yesterday and being fully present in the NOW. Gracefully ageing and giving back what was given to them by the divine, not holding back, and fully expressing God's beauty, and just simply being.

Nature is a great teacher, medicine for the soul, and a playground for the child at heart.

Silent witness - 2015-11-03 20:41

I am always present
I am always near
I am always here
Do not fear
Wipe away your tears
Love is near
I am here
I am here, do not fear

Magic - 2015-12-07 19:39

Magic is what I found in my heart, magic
is my source, magic the day, magic the
night. That some may see it and others
deny it- is of their own concern- because
magic lives, and magic is, in every single
particle of being. But what is being?
Being is bliss, being is freedom, being is
the liberty of truth, the light of the dark
and the dark of the light. What is magic?
I AM!

What do you see? - 2015-12-08 21:43

I see you and I see me
What is within me is also within you
The breath in you is also the breath in
me
The life in me is also the life in you
That which has created you has also
created me
We are one- that is divinity

Sleep - 2015-12-09 12:00

A moment where the soul gets to play
Freedom from the day
A reset button is what they say
Outside our comfort zone
A fantasy
Reality obscured
A dreamer's playground
No rules, just play
A sweet escape from the madness of the
day
Sweet lullaby I say
Goodnight for today

Seconds - 2015-12-10 18:39

What is a second?
It is in the eye of the beholder I say.
For a child at play, it is an entire day.
For the unfortunate man 'tis an unending day.
What is a second?
A mere moment of eternity's work at play.
It is the seedling popping out in May.
The last of the sunlight's ray.
What is a second?
The hair on an elder's head turning gray.
The woman weeping in great dismay.
And the moment she begins to pray.
What is a second?
You are the second.
You are the second, the first, and the third.
You are what you sought now, before, and after.
The second is you.

What is freedom? - 2015-12-12 19:29

Freedom is joy, a soft kiss, a whisper in the ear, the cry of a newborn child.

Freedom lives in the hearts of those who live fearlessly in a world where truth is shunned.

Freedom is choice, a great dancer, the feather in the air, neither here, neither there.

Freedom starts in the heart of the ones who see what the eyes cannot speak.

Freedom is love, kindness, a time that does not exist, something on someone's list.

Freedom evolves out of the nothing from where it is born and slowly begins to transform.

Freedom is breath, the polka dot dress, the man with dreads, and an old man's death.

Cold - 2015-12-25 17:50

She feels a little cold,
You see, she overcame the storm, the
long days and the dark nights
She waited to see the lights, so she could
feel alright
She held on with all her might and
waited for daylight
Now the struggle is over, it's time to
warm over
Stillness has won her over like a sweet
silent lover
'Move over,' she says, I AM the lover

Dormant - 2014-10-01 18:52

Useless is the language which cannot
define what is divine, useless are the
words that confine, useless the days that
I cannot find you, useless the memories
that do not remind me of you, useless
without you, I cry, and I cry until I find
you.

Divine elixir - 2014-12-05 10:48

Elixir of my heart, I cannot see you.
Elixir of my thoughts, I do not
understand you.
Elixir of my soul, I cannot touch you.
Elixir of my sorrow, I know not of your
tomorrow.
Elixir, my divine elixir, you intoxicate
me with your eternal love; heal my
wounds so I know not of any sorrow, nor
tomorrow.
There is nothing to understand, nor
anything to see, for all I seek, is already
within me.

Blind - 2014-12-08 20:46

I wish to whisk away this blindness so
that I could see what is real, so that I
could feel what is near, so that I could
hear that which I fear, only to find that it
is not real.
I come and go through the forest of this
blindness, only to find kindness, which
is real.
What is fear? It is not real. What is here
is only real.
Through the days and through the
nights I see the light of what is real.
Blindness gone, I feel no fear, I only see
what is real.

About The Author

Maria Velazco graduated from CSULB with a bachelor's degree in journalism. She is a trained yoga teacher and student of life, she has studied various disciplines including Buddhism, shamanism, and Hinduism among others. By keeping an open mind, a closed mouth, and open ears, she has been able to learn from the world around her, this is her first published book.

www.ingramcontent.com/pod-product-compliance
Lightning Source LLC
Chambersburg PA
CBHW071635040426
42452CB00009B/1639